JASPER'S JOURNEY

Written by Barbara Gay   Illustrated by Libby Nickel
Copyright 2018 by Just Fun Books & Things.
4991 Manor Ridge Lane, San Diego CA 92130
All Rights Reserved. Printed in the United States of America.
No part of this publication may be reproduced or distributed in any form or by any means, or
stored in a database or retrieval system, without the prior written permission of the publisher.
ISBN 978-0-9990471-7-0   LCCN 2018913007

Jasper just woke up from his morning nap and is looking around for something to do. He looks around the yard and can't find anything new. Suddenly he sees a rabbit hopping across the yard toward the gate.

He starts chasing the rabbit and is surprised that the gate to his yard has accidentally been left open. He runs out the gate and keeps on chasing the rabbit.

He runs and runs and runs. He can't see the rabbit anymore. He stops to rest and doesn't know where he is. He knows that he is on a country road with very few cars or houses.

He is tired, hungry, and thirsty. He knows that he is lost and doesn't know how to get home.

He looks around and sees a big, white house nearby. It has a fence around it, but the gate to the driveway is open.

He walks up the long driveway and around to the back of the house. It is dark outside now, so he lies down under a table on the porch for the night.

He wakes up the next morning when he hears the door opening. An old lady named Ella comes out of the door. She says "Hi doggie—where did you come from?" Jasper wags his tail and is glad that she is friendly!

She goes back inside the house and brings out bowls of water and food and a nice, soft rug for a bed!

5

Ella then calls the Humane Society to see if they can help her find his home. She says she is old, lives alone, and cannot care for him.

The Humane Society says no one has reported a lost dog. They also have a waiting list of 200 before they can take him in!

She calls the local Sheriff's office to see if he can tell her what to do.

The Sheriff tells her they have no place for stray animals. He tells her to call other Humane Societies. No one can offer any help for Jasper!

Ella calls and asks her son, Dan, and his wife, Linda, if they can come and help her find a home for Jasper.

They take him to the Veterinarian to get examined, shots, and microchipped.

Ella, Dan, and Linda decide to give Jasper a bath after his visit to the Vet.

Dan puts him in the bathtub and scrubs him with soap and water. Then he rinses him off with the shower.

After his bath, Dan dries him with a large towel. Jasper is very happy to be clean!

Linda's sister, Sue, is a "big rig-long haul" truck driver who has been looking for a pet as a companion to ride with her in her truck.

Linda calls Sue and asks her if she would like to adopt Jasper.

Sue is happy that they found Jasper for her to adopt!

Sue is in her truck in another state, so Dan and Linda arrange to meet her in Kansas City, Missouri to give Jasper to her.

Jasper and Sue hug each other as soon as they meet!
They both know they are meant to be together.

Jasper jumps into the truck and tries to get up to the
top bunk. He can't make it, so he settles in the lower
bunk. They start their first trip together.

After a few hours, Jasper scratches at the window to let Sue know he needs to get out to go potty.

She stops the truck at the side of the road, puts his harness on him, and takes him for a long walk.

After they return to the truck and continue their journey, Jasper enjoys looking out the windows at the scenery as they travel.

He likes the views of the country better than the cities. The cities seem to have too many people, houses, and streets for him to see everything he wants to see.

After just a few days of looking out the windows, Jasper learns to push the button to lower them!

Sue knows that is dangerous for Jasper. She is afraid that he will fall out of the truck. After that, she makes sure that the windows are locked all the time.

Jasper enjoys the times they stop at truck stops. He gets to meet and make many new friends.

Jasper gets lots of greetings from other drivers because he is such a different kind of dog! He is a Catahoula Hound Dog, and most people have not seen a dog like him before.

At one of his favorite truck stops, Jasper meets a very small dog named Killer.

Even though they are different sizes, Killer and Jasper play well together. They always look forward to seeing each other at this stop on their travels.

At another truck stop one day, Sue went to the back of the trailer to check on the things inside.

She was inside the trailer when she heard the sound of a window breaking.

Sue quickly got out of the trailer and saw that two men had broken the window and were trying to steal Jasper!

Jasper breaks away from the men and runs to Sue. They both are glad to see each other.

At another truck stop on another day, Sue is walking Jasper when a mean dog runs up to them.

Sue tries to get away from the mean dog. She isn't fast enough, and he bites Jasper on one of his legs.

Sue takes Jasper to a local Veterinarian.

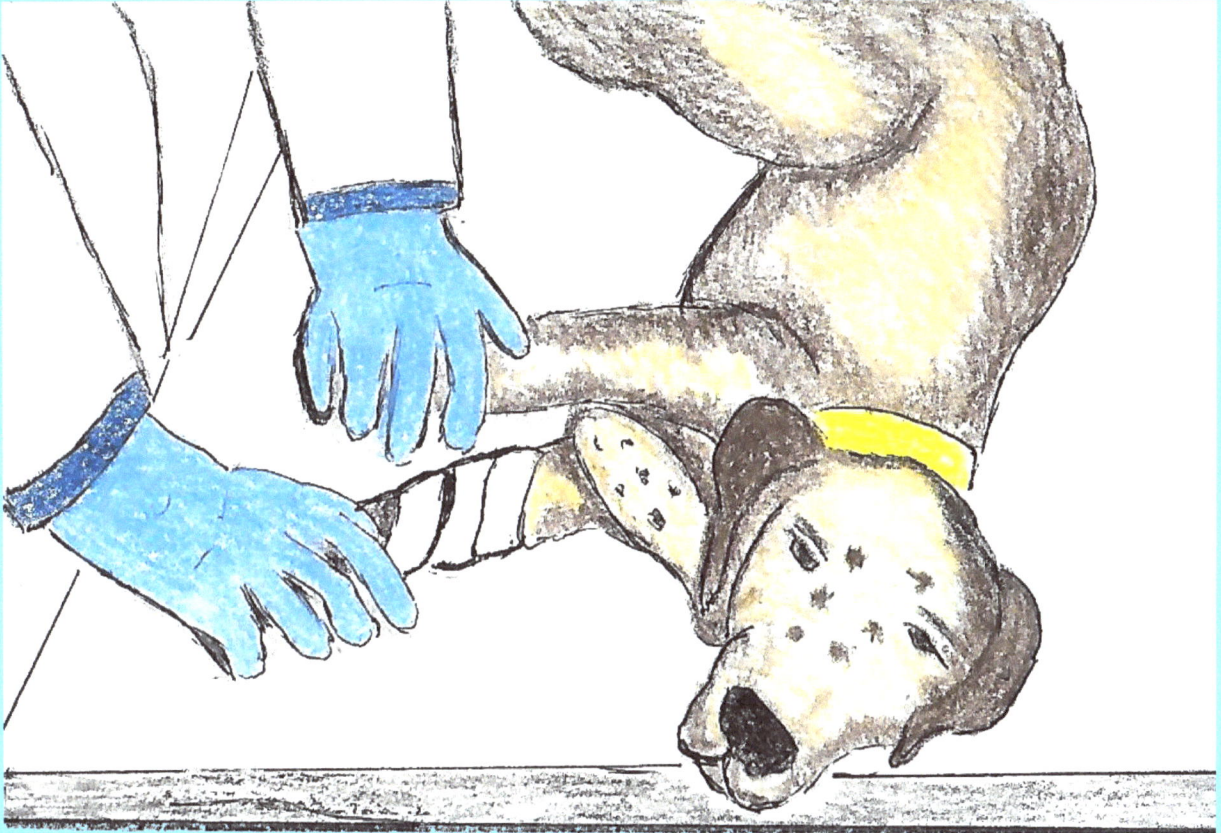

He has a puncture wound on his leg. The Vet cleans
the wound and puts stitches in his leg to close it up.

Since Jasper has to wait to see the Vet again to get his stitches removed, he and Sue go to a motel for a few days. While they are staying at the motel, they get to do many different things.

The first thing they do is to go to a local dog park. Jasper gets to meet other dogs and makes more new friends.

The next thing they do is to go to a pet store. Jasper likes to walk up and down the aisles and see all the different kinds of food and toys.

After the Pet Store, Sue takes Jasper to a doggie day care. He gets to meet and play with more friends while she goes shopping for food and other things.

Jasper is a very happy dog. He feels lucky to have Sue as his owner and to get to travel to many new places he would otherwise never get to see.

For Marcus, Chiara, Sonja, Leilani, and their children.
This book was inspired by the activities of Jasper—a dog who was abandoned, found, and cared for by "Ella" until he was adopted by her son and his family. All names of persons and places have been changed.

Thanks to the following:
    Ray, David, and Astrid for their patience and help to the writer while working on this book.
    "Ella" for her help by providing the details and pictures of Jasper's life.
    "Dan" and "Linda", for getting veterinary and other care for Jasper before he was adopted.
     "Sue" for adopting Jasper and providing him with a safe, loving home.
    All of the Humane Societies and other pet shelters who rescue, care for, and find good homes for all animals who need their help.

For information on other related books or products, contact JUST FUN Books & Things at justfunbooks.com, justfun1936@gmail.com, or by phone at (858)-342-3816.

www.ingramcontent.com/pod-product-compliance
Lightning Source LLC
LaVergne TN
LVHW072102070426
835508LV00002B/230